Poetic Memoirs of a Navigator

Natania H. F. Watie

Poetic Memoirs of a Navigator

Written & Published by
Natania H. F. Watie

Royal House
Publishing

First Print: 2020
ISBN: 978-1-7350446-0-6

Royal House Publishing
Wichita, KS

Dedication
* Te Amo Mamá *

The one thing I'm most grateful
for in this life is my mama.
For the lessons she taught me
for the love she bestowed upon me.

I'm thankful for her introduction of me
to our Creator
most importantly
blessing me with favor.

My love for her runs as deep
as it is wide.
To infinity and beyond
we've vowed to ride.

I love you, mama
for all that you are.
Even for how you handled me wrecking
your car.

There aren't enough words to explain
what you mean to me
so I'll try it in Spanish
to express the joy you bring...

Me encanta su sonrisa,
y no quiero olvidar nunca.

Gracias mamá por darme tú fuerza
Es algo que se mantiene para siempre

Me encanta la escencia que es usted
Eres una verdadera benedición de Dios

Te amo mamá.

Natania H. F. Watie

Poetic Memoirs of a Navigator

* Table of Tales *

* Acknowledgements *

Before I do anything else, I must thank God. I thank
God for everything, for the past, present and future. I
have made many mistakes but I'm so grateful to have
the opportunity to get it right.
Next up, I have to thank God for my parents.
They've given my brothers and me the teaching, love,
and support that we needed. And I am forever
grateful.
Te amo, mamá y papá.
Family and friends – close or distant, I thank
God for you for having helped me on my road of
faith. Whether the lesson was bitter or sweet, I love
you.
Last, but most certainly not the least, I thank
God for everyone who's reading these words. Even if
you find disagreement with them – they had to be
written. At the time they were my private thoughts.
They were my prayers. They were my dreams. These
words I first shared with God.

Poetic Memoirs of a Navigator

LOST

Natania H. F. Watie

* Prologue *

I started writing at a young age; I can date my first stories back to age seven, but it wasn't until middle school that I saw it as a tool. Writing has always been a source of comfort for me. There were days where all I could do was be in my head, feeling every emotion from happiness to dread. Keeping to myself never brought me any solace, but day after day it's what I did to feel safe.

For me, safety meant being free from rejection – in all aspects. I made friends at school for sure, but only at school. I didn't invite them into my home life at all. As for boys, I grew up with four brothers. And being the only girl, I knew I wouldn't be allowed to do much, but even that wouldn't stop my fear. So, I learned to give more of me than what I received, and it became a part of me. I was lost and uncomfortable in my own skin until I grew up and learned to love me. With growth, came wisdom. With hope, came faith. With faith, came love, and the rest is history in the making.

When I put pen to paper, I realized that I could let those emotions out and they would speak on their own. I couldn't do much good with them inside, so I needed them out to clear my sense of sight and perception. Being in my head for so long kept me

from seeing the beauty of my life as it happened. Too
many times, I let my own distorted perception of
myself ruin the beauty that is me. So, one day I
decided I'd be free.

I started to write what I felt in imaginative
ways. I wrote simple metaphors such as "Life is a
rollercoaster," and they became more complex like,
"This life of mine is as rocky as the mountains, yet as
vast and ever expansive as the ocean floor." I learned
to convey my thoughts with imagery that could
pinpoint almost exactly how I felt.

I hope that these poems will show you what
I've felt on this journey. I hope that they tell a story of
redemption. There is a journey for the madness, and
there is hope in the sadness. My story is not my own –
of this I'm sure. I hope that my poems will inspire
someone else to have a relationship with the Most
High and tell their own story.

I'm grateful and beyond blessed to be on this journey.
With God,
I've found my way.

* Surrounded, Yet Alone *

A screaming child stands in the center
No one moves around her
No one comforts
They stare.
She needs something
Nothing they can provide.
She needs it...
The one thing she won't request.

They pity her
As the gods pitied those lonely mortals.
Alone, she begs for it.
A devoted lifeline
A lamb depending on its shepherd
for protection from the wolves.

* August 03, 2016 *
11:27 p.m. On a Wednesday
Cycle

I won't say his name
Because it's probably not true.
I met him as a very young girl
he was the very first boy
I can ever remember liking.
Second grade
Damn.

You might almost think they were made for each
other?
Probably not.

Timing was never our strong suit
I paint over plain truth
While you prove the paint's worth
I hope that by writing this
I can finally let go.

You might almost think they were made for each
other?
Definitely not.

I've always felt like chasing him

Hell, at this point
I've looked to him most
Hoping for the truth that
we occupy the same boat.

What is fate if it never comes?

* The Family Gathering *

The family gathers,
Reminiscing on a life
Well lived before.
The strength
that poured from her veins
like the sun giving life to all Gods
creatures.

The family gathers,
Ruminating; smiling through the pain.
Trying to remember love
and forgiveness is what she taught
what she gave.

The family gathers,
Remembering who she was
But afraid of what she's become
seeing her future – ever diminished
by the decisions of a son.

The family gathers,
Reliving and loving the memories
of someone taken
Someone still there.

* August 04, 2016 *
11:33 p.m. On a Thursday

I was always taught that through Him (God)
all things are possible. Throughout my life, I've come
to know that this above all else is true. Through faith
and work, I've grown to become someone whom I can
admire. A fighter. And I don't mean that in just the
physical sense, but in the spiritual sense as well –
most importantly, in spirit.

A fighter is all I was ever bred to be, and I
knew it from a young age. I was such a dreamer –
always have been, and I may always be. Maybe that's
not such a bad thing though. After all, how can you
succeed in making the best life for yourself without a
dream and God? From my perspective, that's all we
really have.

This week began with faith, and that's how it
will end. The Lord has blessed me beyond all
measure, and I must never ever forget that. Earlier, I
said that I've grown to be someone whom I can
admire. By that, I mean a few things, but the most
important one is that I'm strong. This week, my car
was involved in a hit-and-run accident, and I kept it
together as best I could.

As usual, the walls caved in, but this time I could
still breathe through it. I cried of course, and uttered

words that I took back later. I felt certain emotions that threatened to overtake me, but they didn't. My mind was clear within minutes, and I didn't blow up completely on my family. It may not seem like a lot, but to me, that's progress.

* A Woman Without a Plan as Thought by a Man *

Your face is like the sun
Unfazed it is eternal
there is none
that could ever compare to your mold
Your mind.

You are unchanged by time
So is that sun that dares to steal your shine.
The bell tolls when you near
me.
You're so close that they fear
for me
my sanity,
my truth is on the line.

But they don't know that even gold bends.
My heat with your heart
would melt the sands
into glass.
Though it is beautiful
easily you'd break
you'd fall
for me.
My name you'd call.

<u>* August 19, 2016 *</u>
<u>11:57 a.m. On a Friday</u>

Every day I wake and thank God for another opportunity to make Him proud and bring Him glory.

* While I Slept *

When I was asleep, I didn't know.
I never knew that pain would grow
I thought a smile could change a life,
but found that it was the source
of strife.

Pleasant in nature, I found a friend.
The ship sank quickly
there was no land.
I swam and swam till I could no more
I almost drowned
then I found a door.

Always open, never closed
Some walk through, and others are chose.
To be great or forever rake?
That is the question.
All my life I've learned this lesson.

While I slept I found chains,
meant not for me, but still it rained.
I was asleep and slept
Uncomfortable, yet it I kept.

But when I saw the black hole

I knew I had to let go.
It dared to drag me under
Somewhere uncovered.

While I slept, I knew I wasn't dreaming.

* September 04, 2016 *
03:40 p.m. On a Sunday
What does it mean to be beyond repair, and how do you know you're there?

When I felt myself lying
I knew I was drowning.
Down into the dirt,
where the gutter hurts.

I stay steadfast, bent on destruction
headed for disaster
I keep faith.
Faith, all I have and know to be true
Love in this life is ancient,
a history granted to a faithful few.

When I felt myself lying
I knew I was drowning.
Into the dirt,
where all your love is hurt.

Want me, you want me.
Love me, no not me.
Fuck me, yeah real slowly.

Natania H. F. Watie

FOUND

* The Battle *

His breath upon me slowly consumes my sanity.
His hand, positioned on my skin, ignites the blaze
that threatens
to destroy my judgment.
His words, they pull at my heart.
This tug of war
never ends
I am the leaf that follows the wind's guide.

This man who stands so boldly
takes me over into his profound abyss of carnal
knowledge.
His army invades my castle built of stone
Conquering.
Victorious in their mission.
Like a first-prize trophy, I am his.

"Not in this life," he says
his heart is not for sale.
But without fight, I gave mine so cheaply
I surrendered, capitulated my all
to a charlatan who gave false promises
of happiness.

But, like that phoenix

I will rise from the ashes
of despair.
I am Joan of Arc.
My citadel is not so easily ruined
It is a fortress, after all
with so many hidden
Pathways to sovereignty.

* September 17, 2016 *
N/A – N/A

I've held on to fire for too long
I held the fire
Because the burn felt good.

* Please Forgive Me, For I Have Sinned *

Icarus didn't know he would burn
neither does my heart, though it yearns.
This straight path of faith
holds me.
While that crooked path of hate
wants to control me.

Please forgive me Father, for I have sinned
For living and loving this crime
For all the times I had to try
to get out the truth
to relieve the heaviness of Your trust.

I blush, he sees
And he denied me.
If blue is true
then I'd color him unfaithful
his words are distasteful.

Please forgive me Father, for I have sinned
For living and loving this lie
For all the times I had to cry
to get out the pain
to relieve the heaviness of the rain.

His gift was doom
no room for happiness
only Emptiness
Stress
Confusion.

Please forgive me Father, for I have sinned
Show me Your mercy
Grant me Your peace
Spare my youth
Heal my heart,
so that my days may be long
as I should have known to be true from the start.

* N/A *
N/A - N/A

The essence of me is pure.
This walk in faith,
I've endured.
Though the road not straight
I cannot break.

I rise, I fall
Through the Most High
I received the call.

*A Leader *

She stands, looking over the cliff
"Should I jump head first," she asks
"Or should I start with my feet?"

The rain here seems to never let up
its sharp daggers always pierce
it never soothes.

"Maybe after I've jumped
there'll be a healing," she says,
"I can start over and claim my truth."

She never asked for this
but curiosity is a beast of its own nature
it is a fiend with a hunger that is insatiable.

Still gazing, longing for the peace that tempts her
over,
she smiles and asks,

"But what is truth without lies?
What is peace without chaos?
How can we know one without the other?
How could I be so foolish to ever think that I,
I could be it.

That I could be love.
That I - who has never had much in this life
Bring life to another."

"What is my truth?
Would I know her if I saw her?
Could I fathom the greatness that she is?"

"No.
No.
No, I don't think I could."

"And if not even I can,
what makes them think they would?
His glory, His love, His peace
is all that I could ever dream."

The thought strengthens me.
It weakens they - who would rise against
me.

"Yes.
Yes.
Yes, I can try."

Staring into the waves as they crash, she laughs.
She steps away
turns around
she understands now

Life, especially hers, is worth living
Worth loving
Valued at such a price that she could fathom

Priceless.

"I accept," she says
I will lead by example
I will lead those for me into victory
I will lead.

* October 14, 2016 *
01:09 p.m. On a Friday
Letter for Metejah and All My Beautiful Nieces

I met a girl eight years ago by the name of Metejah Watie. She was the most beautiful girl I've ever met. God blessed me with the opportunity of being the Aunt of such a special girl.

As I honor the Almighty in everything that I do, I promise to always be a healing and loving voice in your life, honey. You deserve every blessing coming to you, so don't let anyone ever tell you otherwise.

You are talented. You are brilliant. You are an inspiration. And most importantly, you are loved. Love runs in your veins, and it lives in your heart. Though things may seem bad, you can always look up. With God, all things are possible, so never limit yourself to what people may think of you. Your true purpose and potential will be found within yourself, and with guidance from the Most High you will unlock it.

Never, for one moment, believe that you are alone in this life, wonderful girl. I have felt this shell on more than one occasion, and it left me feeling broken and unworthy of any love. If you ever feel this way, speak to your situation and reveal that it is a lie. You will never be alone because God is on your side, and so am I.

We are a lot alike – you and I. But in some ways, we are different. Regardless of the cards you're given, Metejah, always try to see the bigger picture. Black women are known for their beauty, strength, love, wisdom, and courage. Even as a young girl, you exude these traits. With care, these traits will only amplify your greatness.

Don't be afraid to be different. As God's creation, you were born to stand out. And though it may not be celebrated in your home – know that you were divinely created. You're a bright, bold, and beautiful Black girl, so don't feel ashamed of it. Learn to love it, even when you're in a room filled with people who don't look like you – always love and defend whom you are and be proud of that. We live in a world that doesn't celebrate or accept us, but don't ever lose sight of the glory that is YOUR people.

In your life, you will face many ups and downs, but if you don't aim too high, you're aiming too low. When you find yourself thriving – don't speak ill of others. Always remember the past because as you've elevated from it, you can also sink back to it. But if you find yourself sinking to a low place, don't stay there. Forgive yourself and others; then move on back to happiness. If you ever lose your way, keep faith – it will lead you back to your greatness.

I love everything about you, from your silly humor and talkative ways to your creative genius. Learn to always love and cherish you, boo. Because when you love yourself – love is drawn to you.

One day, you will be a young woman who starts a career, and you will have a strong husband and family of your own. Raise yourself, knowing that your actions will not only affect you but those whom will come after you.

You are a shining, bright star in my life and many others. Stay with God and build your faith. The sky is not the limit because through The Creator – we are limitless.

* Time to Awaken *

In the time of awakening
do not be afraid.
Change restores balance
in a world full of decay.

The season will be uncomfortable.
Thoughts may get you down
but do not give up
if you seek to wear the crown.

The crown of truth
The crown of youth
The crown of knowing
a time for showing.

Take these lessons you've learned
Apply them, so your blessing is earned.
Forgive but don't forget
for if you do, you'll regret
it.

No matter how long the fall
don't hold yourself to the drop.
Get back up, keep pushin'
don't stop.

You'll know it's time to awaken
Before your soul is taken
to depths unseen
places of green.

Wake up, my jewel.
Wake up, my Queen!

* December 21, 2016 *
02:05 p.m. On a Wednesday

I don't believe I am lonely. I feel love all around me. I don't believe there is a hindrance in my way, but I know that my stubbornness and undisciplined ways have held me back.

Today, I'm saying no more. I'm no longer being held captive to the wants of my flesh. I know what I need, and I have control over the things that I bring to my spirit. I used to be afraid of rejection, and I'd have done anything to keep it from me, but deep down, I thought that rejection was what I deserved.

My dad deserted us. My mother didn't have any time to give us. My brothers didn't want me around in their business, so I felt like all I had was me. Being alone was the norm for me, and the face of togetherness was my lifeline.

I don't know if anyone has ever felt the sadness I've lived, but I wouldn't wish it on anyone. I'm a lover, probably because I never felt I had enough love. I feel it now though.

My life and emotions have been a rollercoaster in every sense of the word. Up and down, back and forth, I've gone away and returned. Now, I want off the ride because I know that I deserve REAL love. That love can come from family and friends, but it has

to start with me.
　On this day, I will love myself unconditionally and
　　　　work toward the plan that God
has for me.

* True Love *

I want a real love with a man.
Not a
I just want you around to hold my hand.
God's love
That binds and circulates
like blood in our
veins.

I want a real love.
One meant for two whole people
Completely awakened in God.
Consummating our oneness
into something
Eternal.

I want a real love with a man
Created for a plan
Who conquers mountains unseen
and believes in his own dream.
He'll stand tall, and he will be firm.

I need a real love.
A challenging love
An uplifting love
A raise the bar, let's go into business love.
I need a forgiving love.

I'll wait for a true love.

* January 15, 2017 *
01:11 p.m. On a Sunday
A Flower in Bloom

A flower in bloom these days is rare.
The need is obvious
but the effort is hard to bear
for some.

Not me
Not me, you see I choose to love
I choose to be open and willing to try
To fly
To bloom
To drive.

I love flowers and what they choose
to represent
New Life.
Another chance to get it right
Like the red rose that ever blooms
Daring to live a life of
Vibrant
Nature
it is my natural stature.

Wild and free, with the promise to always
be me.
I'd love you
and I'd love for you to love me.
We could bloom.
We could be
Us
Ours.

Don't be afraid to bloom
having thoughts of Winter.
It is only then that we may slumber
Awaiting Spring so that we may flower and enter.

* To Be a Lioness... *

You must be fierce,
yet steady.
Able to lead the pack,
when you're ready.

You must have been taught by Queens
who fought when their shit went rouge
Who prayed and preyed
when her King's head was low.

To be a Lioness,
you must press
under duress
the stress
is all just a test
into a higher calling.
To stand for a King,
To be the one on which he leans.

You must be silent,
learn to be gentle.

Gather strength within yourself,
Follow God – it's Spiritual.

You must be driven for the pride.
All for one, you must strive.

To be a Lioness
Is a blessing.
For he is the King of the Jungle
and you are his uplifting.

* January 18, 2017 *
07:55 a.m. On a Wednesday

My last semester as a junior starts today. Yay!
LOL! All throughout this college career of mine, I've
been a stressor. I've stressed and de-stressed to the
point of losing when I should've won several times.
Moving on, I vow to win – to conquer this trial is my
life's goal now.

I will do so with God's blessing. Though my
job wants the best of me, I won't give it anymore.
They don't deserve it, and they do not deserve the
blessing that is me. I promise this semester to put God
in everything that I do, and when it comes to me or a
job – it'll be me.

This year, I plan to get a new job, and that's
what I'll stick to. The plan for my life doesn't end but
begins here. I will conquer mountains unseen and
remain clean – in my thinking, eating, and speaking. I
can do all things this day and the next, if I keep God
first, and let the light in me be seen. But I will keep in
mind that all people don't need to touch my light, and
I don't need to be sucked into theirs.

Thank you Lord, for all your many blessings, and the love you've shown me for all my days passed, and yet to come.

* The Waters of Truth *

Write me a River true
re-right the wrong
call it renewed.

Leave all your burdens in the wake
Graduate to a new level,
let's escape.

Show me an Ocean blue
with deep waters
and misty rains, like the dew.

Trap our love in your heart.
Don't be fooled
Navigate through the chart.

Tell me of this Sea of clues,
whose mysteries conspire
to conceal the truth that is you.

I think of us when I'm hidden
to myself
I always start from the beginnin'.

Let me introduce you to the Fountain of Youth
where hope springs eternal
and the mountains move.

Protect us at all costs.
Command this vessel
and I'll let you be the boss.

Be my Captain
Oh, Captain
In love
Your Maiden.

* February 02, 2017 *
01:47 a.m. On a Friday
Jesus Is a Love Song

Look where I've come to now
You've brought me from miles.

You've brought me so far now
I know You're my tomorrow.

You've strengthened my faith now
I must follow.

I love You, Lord
The End is not tomorrow.

I will follow.
I will walk in Your path.
I can stand today
because you have
made me glad!

Thank you for the songs I get to sing.
Thank you for the blessing
You've been
to me.

I thank You for a life You've given,
for living without joy is not living.

I stand by faith
Walking in Your sight.

My family, You've given
Blood or otherwise
has risen
the truth of Your light.

* When I Knew I Was Woke *

Leave me alone
Let me be
Gone
Get the hell away from me.

Stand over there
your place has gone
with the air moved
Right along.

I woke up
I left
and don't you dare bring it up again
Peace be with you
Don't steal mine
Can't you see you're running out of time?

I'm free; I'm happy.
Got my shine back
So get the hell away from me.
You were a phase, can't you see?

Don't try, you'll ruin it.
It took me this long to grow through it.

Let go of hurt
Let go of pain
I found that these things only drain
Me of my God-given
Essence
but now that I know
forever
leave my presence.

No longer welcome
you cause trouble,
you give little
then take double.

My effort, no more for you.
My Spirit that dwells
has no room for you.
So gone
Let me be.
And please, stay the hell away from me.

* February 26, 2017 *
1:22 p.m. On a Sunday
Not an After-Thought

To be forgotten…
Or all together unseen
is what I feel
on the wheel.

Men, boys, and girls
it's unwritten
the bad seed
they see
Unbeknownst unto me.

An after-thought
Another glance
No one felt to take
A chance
With me
So I breathe
heavy.

My thoughts
Drive me to be alone.

But here I stay
Ready and willing
I want to dance
I'd love to sing.

All my life I've had a dream.
To feel love
Be connected
See me now
Corrected.

STANDING

* On the Road *

I'm something like an expert
I navigate my way until it hurts
To give up?
No
I'd never let up.

Without a map, I make my way
always thinking to live for the day.
Making plans seems useless,
when the road less traveled
produces
more or less
or less or more.
Without my guide it's hard to know what it's all for.

But still, I strive
Never knowing if the tide will let up.
Even though a few roads were dead-ends,
the back road never failed us.

The ways I remember,
the lessons I surrendered
I keep them with me
Every day I want to render:

A new wisdom
given,
A new blessing
unhidden,
I'm grateful
a learned religion.

Stay prayed up and be wise,
and yes,
it is a crime to be led by the blind.
Share your use.
Know your worth.
Keep God with you,
and you won't go in reverse.

* April 20, 2017 *
05:43 p.m. On a Thursday

Of course I'm writing on 4/20! LOL, nah it's all good because it's just another day in the kingdom! I guess I need to believe this way more often. I'm happy; I am genuinely happy! These days, I've gotten it in my mind to think of what God has for me. Today, I realized EXACTLY what God has done for me.

The Almighty has done so much for me and is about to bless me beyond what I was allowing myself to even imagine. It's been almost a year now, and I can finally see all that I am. Every day the Lord is blessing me and I'm thankful. Every day I'm doing my best to remember the promises and where I've come from. I know that I still have a long way to go but I'm excited, and I don't know that I have ever been. I am now and I'm in love. I'm in love with me and God, and that is exciting!

I love you Lord,

Thank you for opening doors that I didn't even know were there. Thank you for putting godly people in my life to get me there. Thank you Lord, for being my strength, peace, and love that resides within.

* Truth Be Told *

Truly,
I'm not confused
I know exactly what I need to do.

Really,
it all just seems like a lot
a lot of wondering,
Mismanagement of what I've got.
All in the name of giving myself
what I've so rightly earned.

Honestly,
it'd be easy to lose compassion
and give morals a second look
most people do this daily
in the name of making eyes look.
Hatred runs rampant in the streets,
for without justice – there is no peace.

Frankly,
I've wanted no part of a struggle.
I was saddened for many days
before I seen the sunshine in the rain.
Helpless no more
I see a way out

there are no doors.

Sincerely,
I don't know if my words are worth reading,
but my thoughts
They're worth redeeming.

Whether I am heard or silenced,
at least these words will illustrate
my heart's climate.

* Vibin' *

I'm not the "in" your face type.
I'm shy
so you can't be fooled
by the hype.

I wear my heart on my sleeve
some people think that I'm mean
but I prefer it to being green
with envy
like a vest
on your chest, it's heavy
and gives no rest.

They say that good things come to those who wait,
but what of those who were late
or moving fast and missed
the sign at half past eight?

I ain't on a revenge quest
Mine is one of redemption.
So, with that being said
getcho ass out the kitchen
you can't handle my truth
and what I'm baking ain't for you.

I'm dreaming
Feeling, learning
Tryna fly to new heights
Imagine me in the night
So bright
Glowing, it's fantastic
Just tryna make it to my mansion.

* May 23 & 24, 2017 *
11:50 p.m. - 06:55 a.m. On a Wednesday

I started brainstorming what I might say in this letter yesterday while preparing my younger brother, Isaiah's birthday dinner. My mother told me to write it all down and give it to God. As I am a writer, I understand what a written word does. It immortalizes what has been said or thought.

First of all, thank you Lord, for all that You have done for me. I wouldn't be whom I am today without the trials and tribulations of my youth. I give You that depressive spirit that tries to haunt me. I give you the thoughts of dependence that I've had for anyone. I give You ALL my personal relationships. I give You my wants to pursue my dreams, career, to be cared for, to travel, and the things I want to accomplish around the city. Even my wants that are not yet mentioned, You know me and you know what they are. I give You my financial situation. I give You my goals, my fears, and my search for a home.

I know that through You all things are possible. No dream is too far out of reach with You on my side.

Lord, I give You all my temptations of this life and urges that threaten to embarrass me. I trust You in all things because You have continued to provide and ascend me higher, Lord. Thank you God, for loving me, for being patient, and merciful with me.

On this day and every day, I give You thanks and praise. I plan to love and live for You for the rest of my life!

* <u>Thoughts.</u> *

I wanted to be with you.
I, wanted to be with you.
I wanted to sleep with you
because to be near you
meant that I'd feel you.

Inside me,
on top of me
in front of me
and behind me.

Curiosity killed the cat,
but I needed you at
attention.
To listen
I keep reminiscin'
bout what could be
What cannot be
What haunts me.

I wanted you to feel me,
make me feel like a woman should
the heat between my thighs you could
Deal me
a Lifeline
Support for a time

or two.

I was impatient.
I, was impatient.
I was a patient
you never spoke
of.
A secret,
your secret.
Whom never stopped to think
it was a problem
to be discreet.

I just wanted you.
Head over hills, I fell
for you.
Tossed and turned
Flipped upside down
Got burned
With the flu
That is you.

Though I try,
I cannot deny
how you've pierced me.
I want so badly to disappear
from thee.

Cause what you give
is sexual frustration
with no real
Gratification.

I wanted to be with you
but now I'm not
Here now
I'm left with thoughts.

* May 26, 2017 *
07:31 a.m. On a Friday
Faith

This morning, God told me
Not to be afraid
of the greatness that is me.
Don't be afraid
of the greatness
that will be.

I found comfort in the love
I have - given and received
My mother raised me strong
and I know that to cry
is not wrong.

It is strength
Strength to let it out
Let it be known
Let it be removed to grow.

I cannot be afraid
because fear is not in me.
I cannot hate
because it is love that moves me.
I have hope and that brings

about faith
this, I keep with me.

Faith will take me as far as I can go.

* Black Brother *

Brothas really don't know what they do
They protect you
Guide you, lead.
When all you want
is for them to leave
you alone.

They lie to little sisters
and prop us up on pedestals.
While baby boy just thinks,
"Boy, did they get it wrong."

It's to be the men
They have to be.
At a young age
Their light turns green.
Protector, provider, caregiver
if he must
Mama knows that he'd never give up!

They received their fathers '
Blessings at a young age
So it must be true,
God's men are you.

Thank you, big brothers

and littles.
You are my God-given
Knights in shining armor
Play pals when I need a friend
Confidante when we broke another vase,
Challenger when I needed to be strong.

I love you,
Black Brother.

* May 28, 2017 *
10:33 p.m. On a Sunday
Real Love

Tonight, I thought about Real Love.
I asked myself if I'd really
know it if I saw it
and I thought
for a second
the answer might be
no.
Then I thought,
Whoa.
How would that go?
Would I be hurt?
Destroyed?
But I bored the thought,
bought the bid that
it could be no.
But I'd still love me.
I'd flourish fully
because,
I love me.
God moves in wonders.
I breathe in the pure sweet thought.
God graces me and hears me
and

Loves me in the way that I need
and
I am free.
Someone told me today
that
before she'd even spoken to the man
whom God had for her,
he told her father
that he planned
to marry her.
I guess that's real love.
Such a beautiful thought
A dream really.

* Rain *

I smelled the rain
before it came
and got excited for the cleanse to come.

Let it pour
give us more
I thought
I'm ready to renew my heart.
I'm ready for the start.

I seen the rain
off in the distance
I knew the arrival
would strengthen
our bond
or dissolve it completely.

Let it pour
I'll give more
and entrust with You
my soul
I sang
and rejoiced
before it remained.

I felt the rain

when it was due
and I grew
with two
twice more
I felt restored.

Let it pour
Let's do more
Let us shine and bring truth
It's for You.

<u>* Rejection *</u>

It's called Rejection
What you think – low self esteem
We see the same thing.

* May 28, 2017 *
10:48 p.m. On a Sunday

I feel determined.

p.s. I need to practice on my cursive handwriting.

p.p.s. Why is it called "cursive?"

* Talented *

My talents are unseen
they're hidden.
Like an untapped forest
it's forbidden.
Outsiders need not try
when my gifts are given
seeing is believing.

Don't cry for me
All my life I've been free.
Free to make decisions
Free to change directions
Free to make mistakes
in order that I might learn
All that is at stake.

Your gift will make room for you
as it is the God in you
It won't leave you
But if you neglect
You,
What can you do?

I am talented
I am crowned within
God has given me something to believe in.

Don't stop me
get out of the way.
God will direct your path
Once you come back.

Be talented
Be great
Spread love
and Leave hate.

* June 05, 2017 *
09:38 p.m. On a Monday

You have to find joy in the times of sorrow, especially in those moments where you were faking it.

Sadness tried to invade my spirit every chance it got, but I had to immediately call it out and change the course. I've been learning this lesson for a while now. I'm learning that whenever any emotion of destruction comes, to remember God, the blessings, and promises.

I don't have any time for sadness, and I don't have any time for overwhelming despair. My God requires this of me. All of me. He requires the burdens, the thanks, the glory, and trust. Man has failed me too many times, but God won't ever leave me.

I asked for peace, and I was shown that it was always there. I asked for happiness, and I was reminded that it had never left me. I asked for joy, and all I needed to do was show it. I asked for love, and all I had to do was feel it.

We're constantly running out of time, so we can't sit around. Take to the path, the guide is faith. God will provide, just you wait.

Poetic Memoirs of a Navigator

* <u>Now, Get it Right!</u> *

I feel like I'm on the Path.
the right one
that I was looking for
but at a space
Lost my place
now I'm trying to get it back.

Problem is
it never left me
I left it
and all I want now is to be at peace
with it.
I care, I care so deeply
and now all I want is peace.

I'm figuring how to write the wrongs
in a way that's right where I belong
Home,
with my mom.
Laughing and praying with my friends
Telling jokes with my brothers.
Healing,
in God's presence again.

Life is beautiful
I'm on the Path.

Life is beautiful
Removed from wrath
Cleared of spite
I will look unto the hills,
for who has given me life.

Who showers me with blessings
and with strength.
It's where I rest.
On my heart I have a testimony
from it, I have grace.

I feel like I'm on the Path
Life is beautiful
Heal and be healed
I have been told
Now, I will share.

* I Just Want to be Free *

I have a lot of goals
I dream big
Always have
since I was a kid.

I want others to dream big too
I want us all to grow.
My mother told me that when their eyes
are on you,
Look at God.
Truth, ya know!

Free
Oh, what it must be
To be free.

I have a lot of talents
of this I know
I always want to learn,
and express my growth.

Free
Oh, what it must be
To be free.

Others should multi-task too
All of us are jewels.

When you look ahead
you're already first
It's pure.

* Epilogue *
June 29, 2017
6:00 p.m. On a Thursday
History

Over the past year, I've had the opportunity to reflect on me and the things that have led me to this point. I've grown in certain places. I digressed in others but I gained a faith that is stronger than ever. I've learned to let go and let God, and it is the best decision I've ever made. I let God in, in a very intimate way. I bared the deepest part of me to the only one who matters, and on the way, I looked to my parents for advice – even my brothers.

I've prayed for three years asking, "Lord, please be with my family tonight, and guide us all into a glorious and beautiful morning." And when I awakened I would say, "Thank you Lord, for waking me up this morning and starting me on my way; for letting me see the dawning and the sunshine of a brand-new day." I've learned to give thanks instead of complaining, and I saw that it was much easier. In those three years, my family has been tested. My friendships were sorted, and my eyes were opened.

Honestly, as a young girl, I said things as if I hated myself. I felt literally broken, but God. Jesus moved on my behalf and God stepped in.

I used to see loneliness when I saw solitude, but those were my most creative moments. As an emotional young girl, especially growing up as an only girl-child in my household – it was tough. I cried so much, sometimes memories feel partly erased. I screamed so loud that the house would shake. But I loved. I gave. I stocked, and I saved. In my moments of solitude I created dolls and made their clothes. I designed the clothes that I wanted in my closet. I wrote dramatic stories. My truest, God-given love was to dance and sing.

Seeing myself as unworthy through other people's eyes marred my view of God. Looking for approval from everyone crossing my path didn't get me anywhere, but I didn't care. I know now that my eyes should have always been on God. They are now, and I can't look away.

When our eyes stray, we miss the path; it's usually a sharp, sudden turn. We miss it trying to please others. We lose it by trying to be what only God can be to another.

God must be your all – I had to learn it a hard way, but I don't regret it. I've met some beautiful souls, and some that were filled with wrath.

Not even a year has passed since I first saw the sun, and life has just begun.
"No te dejo caer jamas." My Lord has said.

Natania H. F. Watie

* About the Author *

Natania H. F. Watie is an up-and-coming author and publisher from Wichita, KS. Born and raised in the Midwest, she's always dreamed of experiencing life beyond the prairie. At 27, Natania has accomplished much personal growth and has faced many obstacles that only drive her passion for writing and storytelling further.

She has served as a dedicated to volunteer to the YMCA foundation and in 2017 became the youngest Community Development Board Member. There she has had the opportunity to give passionate speeches to crowds all over her hometown to encourage participation and donations for programs that help kids who range from elementary to high school ages. During her time working with the YMCA, she established Bilingual Wichita – a program aimed at exciting and encouraging youth to become bilingual to bridge community gaps.

Natania also dedicates her time and effort with the Wichita Branch NAACP, advising their Youth Council on how they can use their voice to create change within the community.

While *Poetic Memoirs of a Navigator* is Natania's first published work, it is certainly not her first endeavor into writing. She's been an author since birth, but self-proclaimed since 19. In 2019 she began a career as a journalist for Kansas' regional, Black-Owned newspaper, The Community Voice.

Through it all Natania has kept God first in her life, and her family at a close second place. God and her mother, whom she loves and cherishes, are among her inspirations in life. Some of her hobbies include writing, strumming guitars, learning Spanish, and her first love – to sing. She is a soprano at her home church called New Zion Missionary Baptist, and it's been that way since she was five.